This journal belongs to:

_____

E.M. Williams Publishing
Baltimore, Maryland

Copyright © 2020 Jasmine Leigh Morse

All rights reserved. No portion of this book may be reproduced without permission in writing from the publisher, except in the case of brief quotations in reviews.

DISCLAIMER
This book is for entertainment purposes only. It is not intended to substitute for medical advice, counseling, or treatment. Any person with a condition requiring medical attention should consult a qualified medical professional. The information in this book is not meant to be taken as expert advice. The views expressed in this book are those of the author alone and should not be considered instructional or authoritative.

Neither the author nor the publisher assumes any responsibility or liability whatsoever on behalf of the purchaser or reader of these materials. Neither the author nor the publisher assumes any responsibility or liability for any loss, damage, disruption, or contrary interpretations of the subject matter therein. Neither the author nor the publisher is responsible for or liable for any adverse effects resulting from the use of the suggestions outlined in this book.

Unless otherwise indicated, all Scripture quotations are taken from the Holy Bible, New Living Translation, copyright © 1996, 2004, 2015 by Tyndale House Foundation. Used by permission of Tyndale House Publishers, a Division of Tyndale House Ministries, Carol Stream, Illinois 60188. All rights reserved.

Cover Design: Make Your Mark Publishing Solutions
Interior Design: Caryberry Graphic Design

Hardcover ISBN: 978-1-7358080-3-1
Paperback ISBN: 978-1-7358080-2-4

For information about the author, speaker requests, or media inquiries, please visit www.jasmineleighmorse.com or email: info@jasmineleighmorse.com. Or, connect with the author on social media:

Instagram: @drjasmineleighmorse
Facebook: Dr. Jasmine Leigh Morse
YouTube: Dr. Jasmine Leigh Morse
Twitter: @drjleighmorse
LinkedIn: Jasmine Leigh Morse, PhD

Heart Rhythms
A Guided Journal for Thriving in Singleness

JASMINE LEIGH MORSE

E.M. WILLIAMS PUBLISHING
BALTIMORE

Hey Girlfriend!

Let's talk about everything, from self-love, dating, sex, and heartbreak, to faith, forgiveness, healing, and wholeness.

I know I'm not the only woman who's struggled in her singleness. And honestly, when I was single, I wasn't okay, and I didn't know it was okay to acknowledge it. I was holding on to experiences and emotions that I never talked about with anyone. Most of all, I lived my life on a timeline, trying to attain what I thought was my peak—career, husband, and family. I was challenged because of the pressure I placed on myself—which led to fear, anxiety, and depression—when my timeline was thrown off by the impact of emotional traumas like childhood hurt and relationship heartbreak. I was also combatting societal stigmas about marriage being the measure of success for women. This person and that person had the world's best advice for how to find, keep, and marry a man. Therefore, I was surviving singleness instead of thriving in singleness.

Yet, with my faith in God, a strategy, and courage, I was able to focus on healing from the pain of my past. When I became laser focused on my wellness with introspection and intentional effort, I started to find just the right rhythm for me to begin thriving in singleness, without fear of being single for the rest of my life. Although I unpack the core strategies I used in my book, *Heart Rhythms: Surviving Singleness with Faith, Know-How, & Grit,* this guided journal highlights some of the strategies I used on a daily basis. Likewise, I designed this journal to be a safe space for single women to share their innermost thoughts, feelings, or emotions. I wanted a place where single women can lay it all out there in order to reflect on where they've been and where they're going. It's especially created for those who desire marriage but struggle with singleness in ways that lead to depression, anxiety, and fear. Lastly, I developed this journal to help single women find their rhythm in singleness by exploring the range of emotions and experiences felt while single and satisfied, single and waiting, or single and dating.

So, before you get started, I want you to know that I'm excited for you and can't wait to see you thriving in singleness with faith, know-how, and grit.

Yours truly,

Jasmine

How to use this Journal

We live in a world full of rhythms. Every day we embrace our personal patterns, flows, or regimens—our life rhythms. These are the repeated patterns of our lives that have movement and sound associated with them. They are shaped by the music we listen to, people we associate with, and our daily activities. It's what we do each and every day with consistency and regularity. Of all the many rhythms we flow through each day, understanding and acknowledging our emotional heart rhythm is likely not at the top of the list. Likewise, the *Heart Rhythms* guided journal for single women is divided into three main sections:

- Love Rhythm
- Healing Rhythm
- Peace Rhythm

These sections represent a small facet of what every single woman needs to understand about herself, think about, or focus on in order to thrive in singleness fearlessly and courageously. Included in each section are:

- Inspirational Quotes,
- Daily Affirmation Prompts,
- Writing Prompts,
- Scripture References,
- Exercises, and
- Creative, Freewrite Space.

You are free to explore this journal at your own pace and within your own timeframe. Wherever you find yourself in your journey as a single woman—just begin.

My only ask is that you begin by setting your honest intentions for using this journal. In a nutshell, tell yourself the truth about what you aim to take away from this journal upon completion.

Contents

Being Single Doesn't Define Me: Who Am I Really? 4
A SELF-ASSESSMENT

Understanding Me in Relationships 7
A PAST RELATIONSHIP ASSESSMENT

Love Rhythm 10
   LOVING ME FIRST
   DATING ME HAPPILY
   GRATEFUL GRATITUDE

Healing Rhythm 68
   HEARTACHE & HEARTBREAK
   TEMPTATIONS... TEMPTATIONS... TEMPTATIONS
   FORGIVING ME & THEM

Peace Rhythm 124
   I'M SINGLE, NOT LONELY
   FEARLESSLY SINGLE
   READYING FOR LOVE

Being Single Doesn't Define Me: Who Am I Really?
A SELF-ASSESSMENT

What are your top five goals in life?

What do you value most about who you are?

What wakes you up in the morning?

What do you need the most every day?

What motivates you?

What inspires you?

Which one of your many skills standout most to you?

Your talents run deep. Which of them could the world benefit from?

What skills and talents do others recognize and acknowledge about you?

What are the top three things people should know about you?

Understanding Me in Relationships
PAST RELATIONSHIPS ASSESSMENT

Reflect on your past relationships by answering the following questions.

What type of person do you typically attract?

What character traits do they typically have?

Describe what makes you physically attracted to a person.

How long does it take you to know that you're ready to be in a committed relationship?

How soon do you fall in love?

What let's you know that you are in love?

How do you show expressions of love and affection in a relationship?

How do you like to receive expressions of love and affection in a relationship?

Do you share your feelings open and honestly?

Describe your communication style.

When disagreements arise, how do you typically explain your thoughts, feelings, and emotions?

Love Rhythm

With love, I'll embrace my authentic self, even my flaws. With love, I'll find the courage to honor who I am and how I show up in the world, with patience and kindness. With love, I'll always tell myself the truth. May I find my path toward a rhythm of sustainable self-love, with intention and due diligence. Always and forever, with love . . .

Fall in love with you. *Self-love* is one of the best kinds of love.

Loving Me First
DAILY AFFIRMATIONS FOR SELF-LOVE

Write seven positive affirmations to sustain your love rhythm every day. Recite them in the mirror daily, until your thoughts, feelings, and emotions align with your words.

"I love me a whole lot."

1.

2.

3.

"I am not perfect, but God loves me still and always."

4.

5.

6.

7.

Frame the life you want to manifest with your words.

LOVE RHYTHM SCRIPTURES

May these scriptures sustain your love rhythm. Read, study, or meditate on them day, night, or anytime in between.

Thank you for making me so wonderfully complex! Your workmanship is marvelous—how well I know it. (Psalms 139:14)

NOTES:_____

_____

_____

_____

Love is patient and kind. Love is not jealous or boastful or proud or rude. It does not demand its own way. It is not irritable, and it keeps no record of being wronged. It does not rejoice about injustice but rejoices whenever the truth wins out. Love never gives up, never loses faith, is always hopeful, and endures through every circumstance.
(1 Corinthians 13:4-7)

NOTES:_____

_____

_____

_____

Three things will last forever—faith, hope, and love—and the greatest of these is love. (1 Corinthians 13:13)

NOTES:_____

_____

_____

_____

Date: /   /

Describe seven things you love about yourself.

Date: /   /

What makes you feel loved?

Date: /   /

What makes you feel unloved?

Date: /   /

Have you ever complimented yourself? Write down 14 compliments you can give yourself verbally for the next two weeks. Then, challenge yourself to write down 14 more. Repeat until you have enough compliments for one month or more.

1. _____

2. _____

3. _____

4. _____

5. _____

6. _____

7. _____

8.
9.
10.
11.
12.
13.
14.

MORE COMPLIMENTS...

Date: ___ / ___ / ___

Reflection
WRITE A LOVE LETTER TO YOURSELF.

Dear _____ :

Open Heart ♥

Write
Create
Do Both

Date: / /

Date: /   /

Table for *one*, please.

Dating Me Happily
DAILY AFFIRMATIONS FOR HAPPINESS

Write seven positive affirmations to sustain your love rhythm every day. Recite them in the mirror daily, until your thoughts, feelings, and emotions align with your words.

"I control my happiness. Not him, not her . . . just me."

1.

2.

3.

"I am happy no matter the circumstance."

4

5

6

7

Frame the life you want to manifest with your words.

LOVE RHYTHM SCRIPTURES

May these scriptures sustain your love rhythm. Read, study, or meditate on them day, night, or anytime in between.

The Lord is my strength and shield. I trust him with all my heart. He helps me, and my heart is filled with joy. I burst out in songs of thanksgiving. (Psalms 28:7)

NOTES:_____

_____

_____

_____

I pray that God, the source of hope, will fill you completely with joy and peace because you trust in him. Then you will overflow with confident hope through the power of the Holy Spirit. (Romans 15:13)

NOTES:_____

_____

_____

_____

Don't worry about anything; instead, pray about everything. Tell God what you need, and thank him for all he has done. Then you will experience God's peace, which exceeds anything we can understand. His peace will guard your hearts and minds as you live in Christ Jesus. And now, dear brothers and sisters, one final thing. Fix your thoughts on what is true, and honorable, and right, and pure, and lovely, and admirable. Think about things that are excellent and worthy of praise. (Philippians 4:4-9)

NOTES:_____

_____

_____

_____

Date: /   /

In the last few months, what has made you the happiest?

Date: /   /

Where does your greatest sense of happiness come from?

Date: /   /

What puts a smile on your face or makes you laugh from day to day?

Date: / /

Define what happiness means to you.

Daily	Weekly	Monthly	Yearly

Date: /   /

Reflection

Top seven reasons to date yourself happily.

1. _____
2. _____
3. _____
4. _____
5. _____
6. _____
7. _____

Top seven self-dating ideas.

1. _____
2. _____
3. _____
4. _____
5. _____
6. _____
7. _____

Open Heart ♥

Write
Create
Do Both

Date: / /

Date: / /

"*I'm grateful* for the glimpses of light in my darkest moments."

- HEART RHYTHMS, THE BOOK

Grateful Gratitude
DAILY AFFIRMATIONS FOR GRATITUDE

Write seven positive affirmations to sustain your love rhythm every day. Recite them in the mirror daily, until your thoughts, feelings, and emotions align with your words.

"I am grateful for the courage to create the life I imagine."

1.

2.

3.

"I even celebrate the small victories in my life."

4

5

6

7

Frame the life you want to manifest with your words.

LOVE RHYTHM SCRIPTURES

May these scriptures sustain your love rhythm. Read, study, or meditate on them day, night, or anytime in between.

I will praise you, Lord, with all my heart; I will tell of all the marvelous things you have done. (Psalms 9:1)

NOTES:_____

_____

_____

_____

Let all that I am praise the Lord; may I never forget the good things he does for me. He forgives all my sins and heals all my diseases. He redeems me from death and crowns me with love and tender mercies. He fills my life with good things. My youth is renewed like the eagle's! (Psalms 103:2-5)

NOTES:_____

_____

_____

_____

This is the day the Lord has made. We will rejoice and be glad in it. (Psalms 118:24)

NOTES:_____

_____

_____

_____

Date: /   /

Describe at least two things you are grateful for every day.

Date: /   /

What are you most grateful for about your life?

Date: /   /

In what ways could you show how grateful you are for someone else every day.

Date: / /

Make a list of those closest to you in your life (e.g., family, friends, and co-workers), and describe at least one thing you are grateful for about them.

I'm grateful for _____	Expression of Gratitude

I'm grateful for _____	Expression of Gratitude

Date: /   /

Reflection

Why is the acknowledgement of gratitude so important for a healthy mindset?

Open Heart ♥

Write
Create
Do Both

Date: / /

Date: /   /

Healing Rhythm

Healing ... it's such a multi-faceted word with many levels and intricacies. But once I find my gateway to begin healing, the possibilities are endless. May I find my path toward a rhythm of sustainable healing, with intention and due diligence.

"Severe heartbreak was the gateway to my identity transformation, and it was a loud, screeching scream that let me know I was ready to completely *heal*."

- HEART RHYTHMS, THE BOOK

Heartache & Heartbreak
DAILY AFFIRMATIONS FOR HEALING

Write seven positive affirmations to sustain your healing rhythm every day.

"I have confidence in God to be completely healed."

1.

2.

3.

"I am not bitter but becoming better."

4

5

6

7

Frame the life you want to manifest with your words.

HEALING RHYTHM SCRIPTURES

May these scriptures sustain your healing rhythm. Read, study, or meditate on them day, night, or anytime in between.

". . . I will give you back your health and heal your wounds," says the Lord. "For you are called an outcast—'Jerusalem for whom no one cares.'" (Jeremiah 30:17)

NOTES:_____

_____

_____

_____

The Lord is close to the brokenhearted; he rescues those whose spirits are crushed. (Psalms 34:18)

NOTES:_____

_____

_____

_____

He heals the brokenhearted and bandages their wounds. (Psalms 147:3)

NOTES:_____

_____

_____

_____

Date: /   /

Describe your first experience with heartbreak.

Date: /   /

When you think about your past relationship heartache and heartbreak, what emotions still run deep within you? Have you experienced any triggers associated with heartbreak?

_____
_____
_____
_____
_____
_____
_____
_____
_____
_____
_____
_____
_____
_____
_____
_____
_____
_____
_____
_____
_____
_____
_____
_____

Date: / /

What activities, people, places, and things make your heart feel safe (i.e., anxiety free, stress free, worry free)?

_____
_____
_____
_____
_____
_____
_____
_____
_____
_____
_____
_____
_____
_____
_____
_____
_____
_____
_____
_____
_____
_____

Date: / /

There are life lessons in every situation. What has heartbreak taught you? Make a list of what you've learned about yourself through relationship heartbreak.

1. _____
2. _____
3. _____
4. _____
5. _____
6. _____
7. _____
8. _____
9. _____
10. _____
11. _____
12. _____
13. _____
14. _____

Date: / /

Reflection
WRITE A LOVE LETTER TO HEARTBREAK.

Dear Heartbreak:

Open Heart ♥

Write
Create
Do Both

Date: / /

Date: /   /

"I am confident in my ability to make *positive decisions.*"

Temptations... Temptations... Temptations
DAILY AFFIRMATIONS FOR RESISTING TEMPTATIONS

Write seven positive affirmations to sustain your healing rhythm every day. Recite them in the mirror daily, until your thoughts, feelings, and emotions align with your words.

"I will make good decisions daily."

1.

2.

3.

"I resist the temptation to speak negatively about my life."

4

5

6

7

Frame the life you want to manifest with your words.

HEALING RHYTHM SCRIPTURES

May these scriptures sustain your healing rhythm. Read, study, or meditate on them day, night, or anytime in between.

Since he himself has gone through suffering and testing, he is able to help us when we are being tested. (Hebrews 2:18)

NOTES:_____

_____

_____

_____

So humble yourselves before God. Resist the devil, and he will flee from you. (James 4:7)

NOTES:_____

_____

_____

_____

Stay alert! Watch out for your great enemy, the devil. He prowls around like a roaring lion, looking for someone to devour. Stand firm against him, and be strong in your faith. (1 Peter 5:8-9)

NOTES:_____

_____

_____

_____

Other references: 1 Corinthians 6:18-20, Ephesians 6:10-18

Date: / /

In what ways are you tempted as a single woman? Were there any consequences for acting upon those temptations? Remember to think outside the box.

Date: / /

Reflect on your temptations and what triggers you to act upon them.

Date: /   /

Write about the ways you attempt to resist temptation, including your successes and lessons learned.

Date: / /

List your top three to five strategies for overcoming your temptations, how you plan to implement each strategy, and how you will measure your success over the next three to six months.

Temptation	Strategy for Overcoming

Implementation Strategy	Success Measurement

Date: /   /

Reflection

What are the pros and cons of not overcoming your temptations? Will there be any lasting effects?

Open Heart ♥

Write
Create
Do Both

Date: /   /

Date: /   /

Forgiveness is for me, not them.

Forgiving Me & Them
DAILY AFFIRMATIONS FOR FORGIVENESS

Write seven positive affirmations to sustain your healing rhythm every day. Recite them in the mirror daily, until your thoughts, feelings, and emotions align with your words.

"I let it go for my own sake."

1.

2.

3.

"I forgive them for any wrongdoing."

4.

5.

6.

7.

Frame the life you want to manifest with your words.

HEALING RHYTHM SCRIPTURES

May these scriptures sustain your healing rhythm. Read, study, or meditate on them day, night, or anytime in between.

But when you are praying, first forgive anyone you are holding a grudge against, so that your Father in heaven will forgive your sins, too. (Mark 11:25)

NOTES:_____

_____

_____

_____

But to you who are willing to listen, I say, love your enemies! Do good to those who hate you. (Luke 6:27)

NOTES:_____

_____

_____

_____

Instead, be kind to each other, tenderhearted, forgiving one another, just as God through Christ has forgiven you. (Ephesians 4:32)

NOTES:_____

_____

_____

_____

Date: / /

Reflect on moments in life when you didn't forgive yourself. Examine yourself and then forgive yourself. Begin with, I forgive myself for...

Date: /   /

If you chose to forgive someone you haven't forgiven today, what could it do for you mentally, spiritually, or emotionally?

Date: / /

**When are you most hurt or offended by people?
How do you respond?**

Date: /   /

Fill in the blanks and repeat as much as necessary in the "Open Heart" section of this journal.

I acknowledge that I haven't forgiven _____
_____
_____

I was hurt or upset most because _____
_____
_____

DECLARATION
Fill in the blanks and read aloud for greatest impact.

Today, I choose to open my heart to forgiving _____
_____ . I can't change the situation, but I can change the way I view it. I acknowledge that they are not perfect and, honestly, neither am I. Despite how badly I was hurt, offended, or upset, I choose to forgive _____
for _____
because I want to be free from the hurt, anger, or pain associated with this situation. I also forgive myself for my role in this situation. Every time I think about this person and this situation, I will follow any negative thoughts with a verbal declaration that I forgive _____
_____ , until my thoughts about this person and this situation are no longer shaped by hurt, anger, or pain. I forgive myself and them!

Repeat this for as many people and situations as needed.

Date: / /

Reflection

Has unforgiveness placed any limitations on your life? In what ways can living a life that embraces intentional forgiveness cause you to live a limitless life?

Open Heart ♥

Write
Create
Do Both

119

Date: /   /

Date: / /

Peace Rhythm

Peace is a precious gift from God. When the mind, heart, and spirit are quieted, there is nothing that can compare. Life offers many highs and lows, but there's a place in God that can be attained that allows peace to supersede troubling times with confidence, hope, and trust in God. May I find my path toward a rhythm of sustainable peace, with intention and due diligence.

Yes, I'm single, and *my future is bright.*

I'm Single, Not Lonely
DAILY AFFIRMATIONS FOR MY FUTURE

Write seven positive affirmations to sustain your peace rhythm every day. Recite them in the mirror daily, until your thoughts, feelings, and emotions align with your words.

"I am not afraid of my future."

1.

2.

3.

> "I am closer to my God-intended destiny and purpose with every breath and step I take."

4.

5.

6.

7.

Frame the life you want to manifest with your words.

PEACE RHYTHM SCRIPTURES

May these scriptures sustain your peace rhythm. Read, study, or meditate on them day, night, or anytime in between.

Trust in the Lord with all your heart; do not depend on your own understanding. Seek his will in all you do, and he will show you which path to take. (Proverbs 3:5-6)

NOTES:_____

_____

_____

_____

We can make our own plans, but the Lord gives the right answer. People may be pure in their own eyes, but the Lord examines their motives. Commit your actions to the Lord, and your plans will succeed. (Proverbs 16:1-4)

NOTES:_____

_____

_____

_____

Yet I still dare to hope when I remember this. The faithful love of the Lord never ends! His mercies never cease. Great is his faithfulness; his mercies begin afresh each morning. (Lamentations 3:21-23)

NOTES:_____

_____

_____

_____

Other references: Jeremiah 29:11, John 14:27, Romans 15:13

Date: /   /

What makes you most excited about your future, despite the promise of marriage?

Date: /   /

Reflect on your challenges and victories from the past three to five years. What lessons learned can you take with you into your future?

_____
_____
_____
_____
_____
_____
_____
_____
_____
_____
_____
_____
_____
_____
_____
_____
_____
_____
_____
_____

Date: / /

Reflect on your life, past, present, and future. Write about why your life is worth living.

Date: /   /

Create a personal vision statement that describes what you want to achieve in the next five to ten years.

"I will provide single women with resources to support their spiritual, mental, and emotional wellness. I will trust my instinct, experience, and passion to serve and support others. I will use my best gifts, skills, and talents to tell my truths with conviction and honesty. In doing so, I will be feeding my soul and fulfilling my purpose."

- JASMINE LEIGH MORSE

My personal vision statement.

_____
_____
_____
_____
_____
_____
_____
_____
_____
_____
_____
_____
_____

Date: /   /

Create a brief personal mission statement that defines who you are and what you want to achieve. A good personal mission statement will help support your personal long-term vision statement.

"To inspire single women to thrive in singleness with faith, know-how, and grit."

- JASMINE LEIGH MORSE

My personal mission statement.

_____
_____
_____
_____
_____
_____
_____
_____
_____
_____
_____
_____
_____
_____
_____
_____
_____
_____

Date: /   /

Reflection

Connect to your vision and mission by vision boarding here.

Open Heart ♥

Write
Create
Do Both

Date: /   /

Date: / /

I thrive in singleness, *fearlessly.*

Fearlessly Single
DAILY AFFIRMATIONS FOR THRIVING IN SINGLENESS FEARLESSLY

Write seven positive affirmations to sustain your peace rhythm every day. Recite them in the mirror daily, until your thoughts, feelings, and emotions align with your words.

"I live a fearless life."

1.

2.

3.

"I have nothing to fear because God is with me."

4.

5.

6.

7.

Frame the life you want to manifest with your words.

PEACE RHYTHM SCRIPTURES

May these scriptures sustain your peace rhythm. Read, study, or meditate on them day, night, or anytime in between.

Don't be afraid, for I am with you. Don't be discouraged, for I am your God. I will strengthen you and help you. I will hold you up with my victorious right hand. (Isaiah 41:10)

NOTES:_____

_____

_____

_____

I prayed to the Lord, and he answered me. He freed me from all my fears. (Psalms 34:4)

NOTES:_____

_____

_____

_____

For God has not given us a spirit of fear and timidity, but of power, love, and self-discipline. (2 Timothy 1:7)

NOTES:_____

_____

_____

_____

Date: / /

What are your biggest fears about being single?

Date: /   /

When you think about being single, what emotions, feelings, and thoughts come to your mind?

_____
_____
_____
_____
_____
_____
_____
_____
_____
_____
_____
_____
_____
_____
_____
_____
_____
_____
_____
_____
_____
_____
_____
_____
_____

Date: / /

What does living a fearlessly single life look like for you?

Date: / /

Make a list of your greatest joys and deepest fears about being single.

My greatest joy as a single woman	My deepest fears as a single woman

Make a list of your greatest joys and deepest fears about being single.

Let joy outweigh your fear.

Date: / /

Reflection

What strategies can you use to live a life of fearlessness? How can living a life of fearless faith lead you to a life of fulfillment, happiness, joy, and peace, in spite of a mate or marriage?

Open Heart ♥

Write
Create
Do Both

Date: /   /

Date: /   /

With *faith*, *know-how, & grit,* I'm preparing for the future I desire.

Readying for Love
DAILY AFFIRMATIONS FOR PREPARING TO RECEIVE LOVE

Write seven positive affirmations to sustain your peace rhythm every day. Recite them in the mirror daily, until your thoughts, feelings, and emotions align with your words.

"I wait patiently on the promises of God."

1.

2.

3.

"I am my future husband's favor."

4

5

6

7

Frame the life you want to manifest with your words.

PEACE RHYTHM SCRIPTURES

May these scriptures sustain your peace rhythm. Read, study, or meditate on them day, night, or anytime in between.

A worthy wife is a crown for her husband, but a disgraceful woman is like cancer in his bones. (Proverbs 12:4)

NOTES:_____

_____

_____

The man who finds a wife finds a treasure, and he receives favor from the Lord. (Proverbs 18:22)

NOTES:_____

_____

_____

_____

Two people are better off than one, for they can help each other succeed. If one person falls, the other can reach out and help. But someone who falls alone is in real trouble. Likewise, two people lying close together can keep each other warm. But how can one be warm alone? A person standing alone can be attacked and defeated, but two can stand back-to-back and conquer. Three are even better, for a triple-braided cord is not easily broken. (Ecclesiastes 4:9-12)

NOTES:_____

_____

_____

_____

Other references: Proverbs 31, 1 Corinthians 7, Ephesians 5:33

Date: / /

What is your role in preparing for your future mate?

Date: / /

What are your relationship deal-breakers?

Date: /   /

What is your vision for your future marriage?

Date: /   /

Have you prayed for your future spouse lately? Write a daily prayer for your future spouse. Consider praying for: relationship with God, family, career, education, ambitions, financial stability, emotional health, physical health, past hurt, and so much more. Be specific!

Date: / /

Reflection

In what ways will marriage add value to your life purpose, vision, and mission.

Open Heart ♥

Write
Create
Do Both

Date: /   /

Date: /   /

www.ingramcontent.com/pod-product-compliance
Lightning Source LLC
Chambersburg PA
CBHW071845080526
44589CB00012B/1111